ChatGPT Business Prompt Playbook:

Create an Online Course using AI

"Become a Prompt Entrepreneur thanks to the best ChatGPT books written by a Human".

Kyle Balmer

Prompt Entrepreneur
@iamkylebalmer

Copyright © 2023 Kyle Balmer All rights reserved,

No part of this book may be reproduced, or stored in a retrieval system, or transmitted in any form or by any means, electronic, mechanical, photocopying, recording, or otherwise, without express written permission of the publisher.

Cover design by: B Street Digital

Disclaimer

FOR EDUCATIONAL AND INFORMATIONAL PURPOSES ONLY

The information contained in this book and the resources available for download through this book are for educational and informational purposes only.

NOT PROFESSIONAL ADVICE

The information contained in this book and the resources available for download through this book is not intended as, and shall not be understood or construed as, professional advice.

EARNINGS DISCLAIMER

There is no guarantee that you will earn any money using the techniques and ideas in these materials. You should not rely on any revenue, sales, or earnings information we present as any kind of promise, guarantee, or expectation of any level of success or earnings. Your results will be determined by a number of factors over which we have no control, such as your financial condition, experiences, skills, level of effort, education, and changes within the market. Running an online business carries risks, and your use of any information contained on this website is at your own risk.

Contents

ChatGPT Business Prompt Playbook:
1

Create an Online Course using AI
1

Disclaimer
4

Introduction to book series
7

What is an Online Course?
23

Structure of the guide
24

Course Topic Selection
26

Course Structure and Planning
44

Course Scripts
54

Course recording and editing
71

Course Marketing
90

Recap
108

Well Done
109

Useful Links
110

About the Author
111

Other books in the series
113

Introduction to book series

AI is moving fast. Extremely fast.

So I want you to do two things:

(1) Follow me on Twitter (@iamkylebalmer): *https://twitter.com/iamkylebalmer*
(2) Subscribe to my free email newsletter: Prompt Entrepreneur *https://promptentrepreneur.beehiiv.com*

Both options will keep you up-to-date and ahead of the game when it comes to AI.

But don't worry. You won't hear me talking about LLM-this and API-that. No tech babble.

My focus is making you money using these new AI tools.

My background is in building businesses online and right now, with these new AI tools, the opportunity is more exciting than ever.

I first stumbled across this power over a decade ago when I started a simple blog teaching people how to speak Chinese. I sold digital-products on that blog and made money on auto-pilot.

Thanks to that blog I've never had to work in a 9 to 5 job.

Ever.

I came out of University jobless and have remained jobless ever since.

In fact, it's safe to say I am unemployable.

Since then I've built multiple online businesses, run experiments and made money from from whatever peaked my curiosity.

Was everything a multi million dollar success?

Absolutely not.

Which brings me onto an important point. Before I tell you what you'll learn…

Let me tell you what you won't learn:

-How to get rich quick
-How to get rich doing no work
-How to make passive income doing no work

My point is this…

Everything I reveal in my Prompt Playbooks takes dedication and a commitment to turn knowledge into action.

Are you committed to learning and taking action?

If the answer is yes you are already ahead of the game.

Most people have a fixed mindset, are entitled and want everything now. That's not you.

If, like you, you have a growth mindset, take total responsibility and understand the journey is the reward (not just the destination) then we're good to go.

I'll take the fact that you are still reading as a positive sign!

In which case I'll share with you the good news. Seriously good news:

Now is the best time to start an online business.

When I started out in entrepreneurship things were different:

-You needed technical knowledge (think setting up your website, email system and SEO system).
-You needed a miracle (or lots of cash) to get someone to visit your website (social media didn't exist in its current form).
-You needed thousands of pounds to hire specialists (Want a website that takes payment and hosts courses? "That'll be $10,000 please").

-You needed to attend seminars (my old mentor used to fly from the UK to the US every time he wanted to learn a new strategy).
But things have changed.

> *"The democratization of technology allows anyone to be a creator, entrepreneur, scientist. The future
> is brighter" - Naval Ravikant.*

In other words the barrier to entry is as low as it's ever been. And you don't need anyone's permission to get started:

-Technology is low cost (Software as a service SAAS and No-Code tools means you can launch a business for the price of a gym membership).

-There are multiple ways to drive customers to your website (Facebook, Instagram, TikTok, YouTube, Twitter, SEO and more).

-The knowledge you need is everywhere (Low cost playbooks like the one you are reading, free email newsletters like Prompt Entrepreneur, YouTube videos, Twitter threads, $12 books…)

And the big one…

Artificial Intelligence. More on this shortly…

So let's agree:

The only thing stopping you from starting an online business getting started and following a solid Playbook.

You've already given me a commitment to learning and taking action. And you are reading my Playbook. The only thing left is implementation - getting it done.

Do that and there's nothing stopping you from making your dreams a reality.

Now let's talk about what you'll learn:

The power of AI

I've always wondered why more people didn't start an online business:

-Travel the world
-Work from anywhere
-Have autonomy over your time

Here are some numbers.

Let's say I wanted to give myself a pay rise. In a job I'd have to work extra hours, compete for promotion or do overtime.

In reality I might get a 2-4% pay rise.

If earning $100k a year that's another $4,000 a year. Maybe $150 a month cash in my pocket after taxes.

And for that extra 4% or $150 a month my employer would expect me to grind.

Grind hard.

In comparison here's how I give myself a pay rise. Let's take my Chinese language learning business.

I could launch a premium language product. I'd create a very valuable digital bundle of video courses, PDF guides and printable wall charts. I would probably throw in a bonus gift to help their children learn Chinese.

Let's say I price it up at $50/month.

I'd only need to sell THREE of these courses to increase my income by $150/month.

But I wouldn't have to grind like I would in my job. I would make the programme once and sell it again and again.

And I'd sell a lot more than just three copies...unlike 9 to 5 work the product I've made is scalable. I can sell 1 or 1000 copies without any additional cost to myself in time or money.

You are likely thinking "that's OK for you Kyle. But I don't have that kind of time".

Here's the best news you'll hear all year: the beauty of this is you don't need to quit your job to make this happen.

Thanks to AI.

Artificial Intelligence is like having a research assistance, copywriting assistant, strategy assistant, creative assistant, graphic design assistant, coding assistant, sales assistant, customer service assistant, marketing assistant and more...

For the price of a couple of coffees (and in most cases totally free).

AI let's you start a business in your spare time for very little upfront investment.

But only if you know how to use it.

What you'll learn in my Prompt Playbooks

Everyone of my Playbooks has one universal mission...

To transform you into a PROMPT ENTREPRENEUR.

As a Prompt Entrepreneur you'll have the power to start and grow businesses by leveraging the power of AI.

Together we'll transform you into a Prompt Entrepreneur by achieving these four goals:

Goal 1 - Start an online business with AI

The end destination is the same. Make money online.

The playbooks are like Google Maps giving you step by step directions on how to get there.

So the routes might change (For example: Affiliate Marketing Blogs, Email Newsletter Business, Course Creation, AI Customer Service Bots, Consultancy, Kindle Publishing etc.) but the destination remains the same.

By the end of each Playbook you'll have the foundations of a functioning income generating business.

Goal 2 - Learn about AI

Along the way I'll teach you how to use AI to start a business faster and cheaper.

You'll be on two parallel learning paths

Path one — learning the step by step process and thinking required to launch an online business.

Path two — learning about how to use AI in everyday life and business.

The AI skills you learn from following the Playbook will be applicable outside of what we cover in these pages.

You'll be able to extrapolate what you're learning and start to solve your own business problems with AI.

Think of the business we're setting up as a "live project" that you're using the really get to grips with AI.

Goal 3 - Speed, speed, speed

In the past I could take anyone from no idea to launching a business in 30-days.

It was a book and programme called it '30-Days of Doing'.

The basic idea was to take someone through 30 days of tasks, helping them build a business.
AI changed this.

These Playbooks can now take anyone from no idea to launching a business in 7-days.

Less, if you've already worked through one Prompt Playbook.

That's 7-days, 1-2 hours a day. Or one whole Sunday.

If you have less than one hour a day then give yourself longer time horizon to launch. Don't worry - it'll still be faster than the pre-AI days!

Goal 4 - Low risk

If you tell your mum, friend or uncle you're starting a business they'll likely say "Oh that's risky".

And I agree. Starting a business is risky.

IF: you spend 6-months working on an idea, write a business plan, get a loan from a bank, open up a shopfront and then hope and pray.

Then yeah, I agree - that's risky!

We're not doing that.

Instead I'll be sharing with you online businesses you can start with little to no upfront capital.
But this isn't 100% risk free. There is risk. There's risk in every action we take or don't take.

Here the risk is your time investment.

And I am grateful you are investing your time to learn with me.

It's all possible thanks to AI

The above goals are absolutely achievable if you know how to use AI.

More specifically knowing how to talk to (communicate) AI.

But like all new things, the window of opportunity is small. The technology is evolving rapidly. I want you to ride the wave and reap the rewards.

Don't sit on this. At worst you'll give it a go and learn how to use these new AI tools.

At best you'll launch an AI online business that generates you an income.

Why am I giving away this information?

I believe that everyone has the ability to harness the power of the internet to make more money, find more joy and live a life of purpose.

My purpose is to create, experiment and then share what I've learned.

I basically love teaching.

I've built and sold a TV station, I've travelled to more countries than I can count and built a marketing agency that's handled $1.4 million per year in advertising revenue.

Even after doing all that I find myself here. Writing to you about how to start an online business. I guess it's a calling.

But don't get me wrong. I'm not running a non-profit organisation.

Here's my business model so we both know where we stand:

-I produce high-value actionable information

-Most people consume it for free to low cost (like the Playbook you're reading now which, on Amazon, is priced as low as it can be)

-Some people purchase my more advance programmes, cohort coaching, private group access etc.

Yet I don't create courses for the sake of it. I only release something when I believe it's valuable to you.

The last course I released was in 2019:

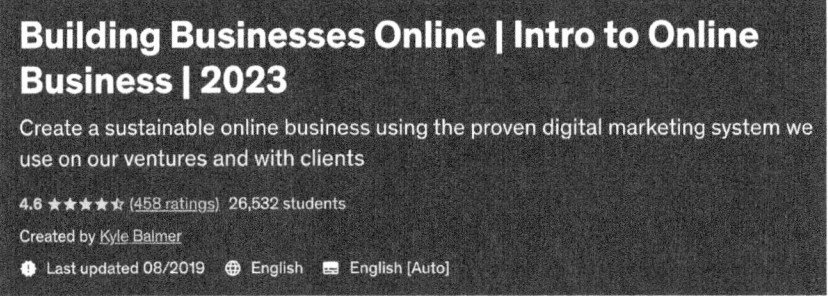

The reason I am back and creating this new series of Playbooks is…

I'm betting on the power of AI.

When i released my last programme in 2019, people still had blocks:

-Fear, "What if I fail?"
-Knowledge, "This is too complicated"
-Time, "I work 50-60 hours a week"

I believe (and you will too after reading this playbook) that AI will smash those blocks to pieces. There will be nothing holding you back from starting an online business and building a life you want.

But when that happens — The self-proclaimed 'Gurus' appear. The 'sharks' appear. The 'make $10,000/month passive income 30-days' guys appear.

In fact, they are already here. A friend attended an 'AI business' seminar in the UK in March 2023. She was pitched a $30,000 AI-business-in-a-box programme. By an AI expert…

The first public appearance of widely accessible AI came in the form of ChatGPT — in NOVEMBER 2022.

It apparently only took this dude 5-months to become an AI expert and sell $30,000 programmes!

What's my point?

I'm not an AI expert. No-one is an AI expert. It's NEW.

Instead I'll show you what I do and we'll figure this out together.

Remember, my playbooks have you on two learning journeys:

Path one — learning the step by step process and thinking required to launch an online business.

Path two — applying the power of AI to path one. Which brings me onto what I do…

The Prompt Entrepreneur Way

Prompt is the fancy word used to 'ask AI to do something'.

Simply put I'll help you *talk to* AI.

I do this through these Playbooks, my free email newsletter and my Twitter profile.

Remember to subscribe and follow.

But whilst you're here let's focus on the Prompt Playbook.

My Playbooks follow a simple structure:

(1) I'll explain the theory of the business model (and the end game)
(2) I'll present you with the steps (what to do, in what order)
(3) I'll give you a Prompt each step of the way (what to say to AI)

(4) I'll show you the Prompt Output (what the AI produced for me)
(5) I'll give you Prompt Tips (how to adapt the original prompt for your own unique business).

My email newsletter and Twitter are additional resources for you. The main benefit of them is speed - AI is moving fast (too fast!) and the newsletter and Twitter account are good places for you to keep up to date with what's happening.

The focus of both is on how you can use AI to start businesses, just like the one discussed in this Prompt Playbook.

So if you like this Playbook you'll love my newsletter and Twitter.

(1) Subscribe to my free email newsletter: Prompt Entrepreneur: https://promptentrepreneur.beehiiv.com

(2) Follow me on Twitter (@iamkylebalmer): https://twitter.com/iamkylebalmer

A Tip and a Gift

A tip:
Think of AI as high-performance sports car.

Put garbage fuel in. You'll get garbage performance out.

Put the best fuel in. You'll get the best performance out.

I'll be showing you how to put the best fuel in to get the best performance out.

A gift:

I share a lot of prompts in this book.

But it'll be annoying to copy and paste them from the e-book version.

I tried and found it super frustrating!

So I've made this very playbook you are reading available here: *https://tinyurl.com/4ec7c5cm* .

This will make it easy to copy and paste any prompt you want to use.

Keep this link private please. I can't stop you sharing it but I'm trusting you not to.

I'm sharing it with you to help you launch your online business even quicker.

Let's get started.

What is an Online Course?

With this business model you package up your expertise into a course which you sell to people who want to learn from you.

Structure of the guide

Over this playbook we're going to go into detail about:

Part 1: Course Topic Selection
Part 2: Course Structure
Part 3: Course Scripts
Part 4: Course recording and editing
Part 5: Course marketing

We're going to be focusing on Udemy in particular, but these lessons are more widely applicable to Coursera, Skillshare, Youtube or self-hosting your own course.

I'm focusing on Udemy because it has the largest learning base. We're going to be tapping into that existing audience of learners rather than building an audience from scratch.

Also, this is the platform I've personally had the most success on and so am therefore most qualified to talk about. Better than me making stuff up!

Here's one of my courses on Udemy which has 26,000+ students and 4.6 star average review on 458 ratings.

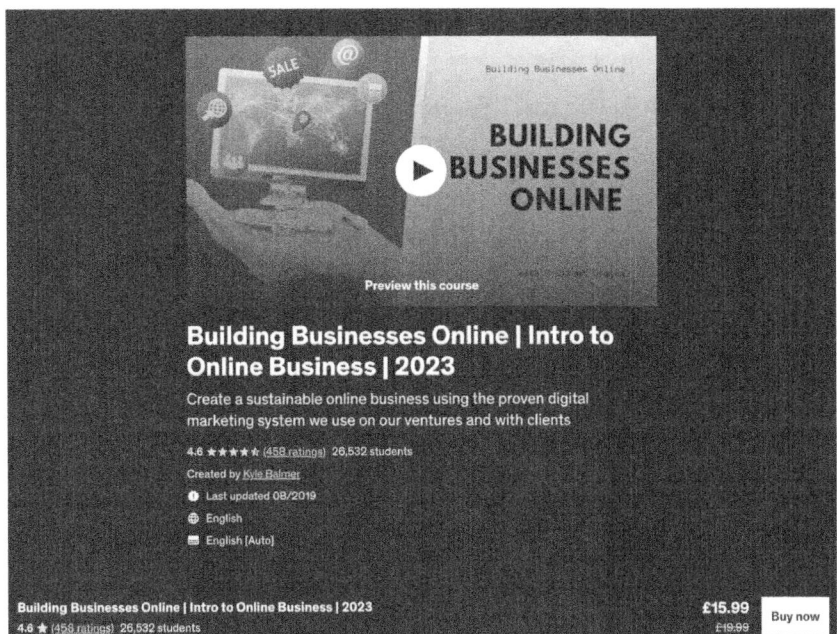

Once you've created your course though you can test it out on different platforms. Or publish it on multiple platforms - just make sure to check the T&Cs on each platform for exclusivity clauses.

Course Topic Selection

In this part we're going to focus in on what exactly your course is going to be about - the topic and your particular unique selling point.

1. Topic brainstorming

You could create a course about something you don't know anything about.

AI will allow you to do this.

However, the end result will be uninspired, dull and probably full of errors!

Instead we're using AI to help us with the process of creating a course - not to do all of the work for us! Therefore the course we are creating should be a topic that we have both knowledge and skills in.

You may already know what this is. If so great; skip to the next step. But if you are at a loss we'll use ChatGPT to help come up with ideas.

Let's start with a simple prompt to start thinking about topics.

> *Act as an online education specialist.*
>
> *I am preparing an online course and want assistance with the course ideas.*
>
> *My areas of expertise are in: [insert skills/ knowledge]*
>
> *Generate 10 unique course ideas related to each area of expertise.*

Please also suggest a key learning objective for each course..

Where the prompt says [Insert skills/knowledge] add as many of your areas of expertise as possible.

The more you add the more ideas ChatGPT will throw at you.

These can be professional expertise from your work or more personal skills and knowledge from hobbies and interests. Don't limit yourself at this point - we want to go wide and get the creative juice flowing.

Prompt Output

Here is an example output for "digital marketing" which is one of my areas of expertise.

> **Digital Marketing:**
> 1. **Course Title:** "Search Engine Optimization (SEO) for Business Growth"
>   - **Key Learning Objective:** Learn SEO techniques to increase website visibility, drive more organic traffic, and grow your business.
> 2. **Course Title:** "Data-Driven Marketing: Analytics for Strategy Development"
>   - **Key Learning Objective:** Understand how to leverage data and analytics to inform marketing strategy, optimize campaigns, and improve return on investment.
> 3. **Course Title:** "Social Media Marketing: Building Brand Awareness and Engagement"
>   - **Key Learning Objective:** Understand the strategies to use social media effectively for brand awareness, customer engagement, and lead generation.
> 4. **Course Title:** "Content Marketing: Driving Traffic and Building Authority"
>   - **Key Learning Objective:** Learn how to create, distribute, and measure high-quality content that attracts and retains a clearly-defined audience.
> 5. **Course Title:** "Email Marketing: Strategies for Customer Retention"
>   - **Key Learning Objective:** Understand how to design and implement successful email marketing campaigns for customer acquisition, retention, and loyalty.

Note the multiple topics here: SEO, data-driven marketing, social media marketing, content marketing, email marketing etc.

These are the sort of topic ideas we want to extract and use in the next step. So note down any that are of interest and we'll be finding out which are good course ideas to pursue.

2. Udemy Instructor Insights

Once you have a handful of potential course topics in hand we need to check how the market looks.

It's not enough to build a course that we are interested in. It also needs to be something that:

- Has lots of interested learners
- Has competition we can beat

For this we'll use Udemy's Marketplace Insights tool. You'll need an Instructor's account on Udemy to do this. This is free and quick to set up here. Go ahead and make an account.

Once you are in your instructor's account go to Tools > Marketplace Insight tool. You'll see a search bar like this:

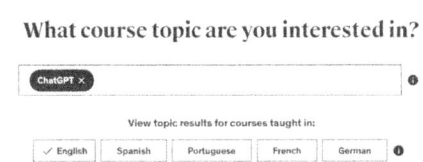

Go ahead and type in one of the topics from step one. Chances are it's a topic on Udemy - if not try variations of the word and you'll find it. Udemy has a huge range of topics.

You'll be presented with a HUGE amount of information about the topic.

For the topic "ChatGPT" for instance I can see that demand and competition is high. Unsurprising considering the top teacher makes $65,000/month.

I can also see the top keywords people use to find the content as well as related topics:

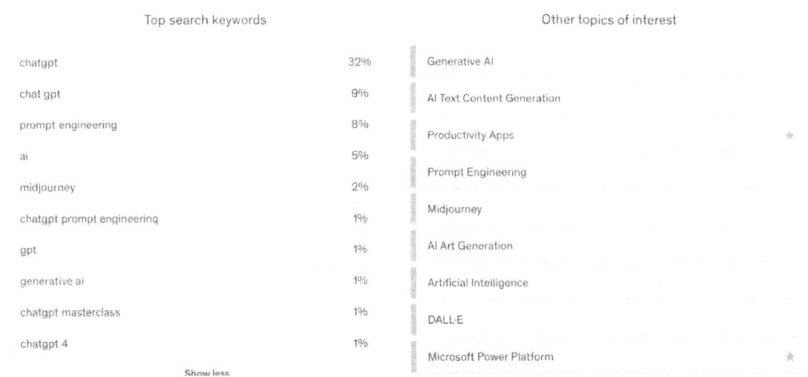

Make sure to investigate those other topics if they are relevant to your skills. Especially those with stars - those have high demand and low competition.

Further down the page you'll also be shown the top courses in the topic, their number of sales and their average review ranking.

Lots and lots of valuable market information that we"ll be using to decide our topic.

Right now go through your topic list from step 1 and look for high demand topics that (ideally) have low or medium competition. These will be the sweet spot.

Collect up a few of these as your shortlist. Feel free to choose a topic now or continue to the next step with a few options if you are still uncertain.

3. Competitive analysis

Once you have one, or a small handful, of topics we want to do some competitive analysis.

This process takes some time so ideally do it with less than 5 topics.

In Udemy's Marketplace Insight tool scroll down to the Top Earning Courses section. You should see 5 courses here. These are the most successful and the ones we want to emulate.

Open up new tabs/windows for each course.

> Act as a course creation strategist.
>
> I will provide you with the details of 5 courses around [topic]
>
> Review each of these courses and output in a table a competitive analysis
>
> The columns are:
>
> - number of students
> - - number of reviews and star rating
> - - length of course in hours
> - - relative strengths of course
> - - relative weaknesses of course -
> - unique content in this course not available in other courses

- *I will provide 5 courses worth of details. Please prompt me for each course one at a time until you have all five and then perform the analysis.*

For each course copy/paste the:

- What you learn
- This course includes
- Description

The description text may be too long for ChatGPT to process. If so take the first few paragraphs as they should be the most important.

Prompt Output

Make sure to add in the [topic] in the prompt and hit enter.

ChatGPT will then ask for details for each of the 5 courses.

If you provide information but ChatGPT is still missing info it will prompt you for more.

Keep going until you've added information about all 5 courses. Then ChatGPT will begin its analysis. It may need to be told to begin the analysis after the 5th course- just say "start" or "ok" and it'll begin.

The output will look like this:

Course	No. of Students	No. of Reviews & Star Rating	Length (Hours) & No. of Lectures	Relative Strengths	Relative Weaknesses	Unique Content
Course 1: ChatGPT Complete Guide	75,044	9,388 reviews, 4.6 rating	14 hours, lectures not specified	Comprehensive coverage of AI tools; Hands-on exercises	Could be overwhelming for beginners; Some parts might need programming knowledge	Multimodal use of AI tools; DALL-E 2
Course 2: The Complete Guide to ChatGPT & OpenAI APIs	21,031	1,836 reviews, 4.7 rating	12 hours, lectures not specified	Focus on ChatGPT and OpenAI APIs; High rating	Might be a bit advanced for beginners; Less hours compared to others	Integration of OpenAI's APIs into custom code; AutoGPT and LangChain
Course 3: ChatGPT Guide for Beginners to Experts!	44,118	6,222 reviews, 4.5 rating	9 hours, lectures not specified	Wide array of applications covered; Pro-tips on usage	Might not delve deep into certain topics due to breadth of topics	Use of ChatGPT for SEO, E-commerce, translation; Academic use of ChatGPT
Course 4: Build Solutions and Apps with ChatGPT	20,988	2,179 reviews, 4.5 rating	6.5 hours, lectures not specified	Focus on creating applications and integrations	Fewer hours; Could use more theoretical backing	App creation with business platforms and no-code development apps
Course 5: Unleash ChatGPT and GPT4	11,394	859 reviews, 4.8 rating	13 hours, lectures not specified	Detailed content on GPT-4; High rating	Assumes familiarity with Python APIs; Fewer students could indicate niche content	Use of GPT-4; Text embeddings Use of Whisper for audio file translation

This gives us a comparative analysis of the top 5 Udemy courses in our niche.

Because these are the top 5 they are doing something right - we want to learn from them. So this is invaluable information. In the next step we'll go a little further with this competitive intelligence.

4. USP/ Gaps in the market

In the same prompt window go ahead and add this prompt below the comparative table.

If you have navigated away from the previous chat look in your chat history to find the comparative analysis again.

Now use this prompt:

> *Based on the comparative analysis you just completed, propose a course that takes the best from each, and avoids the weaknesses.*

No additional info needed - ChatGPT will take all the information it needs from the comparative table above.

Prompt Output

Absolutely, based on the comparative analysis and understanding the unique strengths and weaknesses of each course, we can propose a course that takes the best from each, and avoids the weaknesses. Here is a proposed course:

Course Title: "AI Revolution: Mastering ChatGPT, GPT-4 and OpenAI APIs with Practical Applications"

Course Highlights:

1. **Comprehensive Coverage:** The course would provide a complete understanding of AI tools, including ChatGPT, GPT-4, OpenAI APIs, DALL-E, and more, ensuring that students get a broad and deep understanding of the AI landscape.
2. **Practical Implementations and Applications:** Drawing inspiration from Courses 3 and 4, we will focus on practical applications of these tools in real-world scenarios including SEO, E-commerce, translations, creating apps, and integrations with business platforms.
3. **Guided Prompt Engineering:** A major focus will be on teaching students to engineer perfect prompts and fine-tune the models' performances, which was a strength in Courses 1 and 2.
4. **Advanced Concepts Simplified:** Our course will cover advanced topics like text embeddings and whisper for audio files, similar to Course 5, but will make sure to present them in a simplified way that can be understood even by beginners.
5. **Hands-on Approach:** Like Course 1, this course will also focus on hands-on learning, with many exercises and practical projects that allow students to apply what they've learned.
6. **Beyond Theories - Real-world tools:** We will provide tutorials on how to integrate these tools into no-code platforms and popular business platforms. This feature, inspired by Course 4, will empower students to apply their knowledge in real-world settings.
7. **Pro-tips and Tricks:** Inspired by Course 3, we will provide pro-tips and tricks on usage, which would come from experienced industry professionals.
8. **All-levels Welcome:** This course will be designed in a way to cater to both beginners and advanced students. The content will be broken down into digestible sections with clear learning paths for different student profiles.
9. **Community and Continued Learning:** Students will have access to a community forum for course-related discussions and doubt resolution. Regular updates and additional resources will be provided for continued learning beyond the course.

By combining the best elements of each course and addressing the weaknesses, we aim to create an industry-leading course that is comprehensive, practical, accessible, and keeps students engaged and empowered.

This prompt takes all of the competitor information you provided, all the strengths and weaknesses, and suggests a course that is *better* than the others.

We will use this list of highlights later when we come to structure the course. So make sure to keep a copy.

5. Course title

Next we want a handful of potential titles for our course.

Use this prompt:

> *Provide me 10 more potential titles.*
>
> *Try to include keywords from this list, ordered from most to least important: [keywords]*

For the keywords refer back tot the Udemy Marketplace Insights tool and the top search keywords.

Top search keywords

chatgpt	32%
chat gpt	9%
prompt engineering	8%
ai	5%
midjourney	2%
chatgpt prompt engineering	1%
gpt	1%
generative ai	1%
chatgpt masterclass	1%
chatgpt 4	1%

Prompt Output

Sure, based on the keywords you've provided, here are 10 potential course titles:

1. "ChatGPT Masterclass: Unleashing the Power of Generative AI through Prompt Engineering"
2. "Beyond AI: Advanced Prompt Engineering with ChatGPT and Midjourney"
3. "The Ultimate Guide to ChatGPT: Master Prompt Engineering & Midjourney in AI"
4. "Demystifying AI: A Comprehensive Guide to ChatGPT, Midjourney, and Prompt Engineering"
5. "Transformative AI: Understanding ChatGPT and Generative AI through Prompt Engineering"
6. "ChatGPT & Midjourney: The Future of Generative AI and Prompt Engineering"
7. "Navigating the AI Landscape: Prompt Engineering with ChatGPT and Midjourney"
8. "Prompt Engineering Mastery: Unleash the Full Potential of ChatGPT and Generative AI"
9. "Exploring AI Frontiers: From ChatGPT to Midjourney, Prompt Engineering and Beyond"
10. "AI, ChatGPT & More: A Practical Guide to Prompt Engineering and Midjourney"

These titles aim to capture the depth and breadth of your course while highlighting the key themes you've identified.

Choose one that includes the keywords but also *sounds* good. You'll be better than ChatGPT at choosing this.

Pulling it together

Phew!

In this part we started with idea generation, worked through market and competitive research and came out the other side with a set of guidelines for the "perfect" course as well as a name to go along with it.

That's a lot of work done. In fact, the most important work.

We're going to build on these elements, especially the set of guidelines for the perfect course, in the next Part as we start to structure and write the course.

Course Structure and Planning

In this part we're going to be focusing on structuring and planning our online course.

This is a big and complex task but I've written an equally big and complex prompt to do the heavy lifting for you.

1. Length of course

Before we beginning structuring everything we need to know the length of the final course.

First question: do you want to make the course free?

Why would you want to make it free?

If you have other products/services or simply want to build up an audience then you can use a free course on Udemy to get to a lot of people. Then you take them from the course over to your social media and email list and sell them your other products and services.

Making the course free gets it into the hands of the most amount of people - thus driving your other business further down the line.

If you want to do this then the course has to be under 2 hours. That's the limit for free courses on Udemy. So your course length should be 2 hours.

Don't want the course to be free? No problem - here are the next considerations.

If you want the course itself to be the income generator then you can have any length of course.

If this is the case look at the length of the top selling courses in your Topic and replicate this.

In AI for instance they are all around 15 hours so for a paid course I'd go for around 15 hours.

A caveat to this : if your competitive analysis and perfect course guidelines (from Part 1) came up with suggestions to make your course longer or shorter then follow these suggestions.

The final thing to keep in mind is your time. A longer course will take longer to make- obviously! If this is your first course think about keeping it shorter at a couple of hours rather than a marathon 20 hours course!

In any case, for this step come up with a final number for how long you want the course to be. We'll be using this to help structure the course.

2. Structure prompt

Using all of our work so far we can now plug into this chunky course structure prompt. I'll work through it piece by piece after so you understand what's going on here.

Use this prompt in your existing chat that contains data on the 5 competitor courses you analysed.

Why? Your perfect course guidelines will likely refer to the 5 competitors so use the same chat so that ChatGPT has sufficient context:

> *Act as an online course expert*
>
> *I'm preparing a course about [topic]. You will decide the Sections and Lessons this course will contain and build a course structure.*
>
> *The course title is [title]*
>
> *The total length of the course should be [total length]*
>
> *The course structure should be split into Sections, each section containing multiple Lessons. Adjust as necessary to fulfill the total course length. Each section should end in a Quiz.*
>
> *Each lesson should be no more than 10 minutes. There should be 5-8 minimum lessons per section. Split the sections into*

multiple lessons accordingly, making sure to hit the total course length.

Make sure that the total course length adds up to the total length provided above.

The course structure should follow these guidelines

#begin perfect course guidelines#
[paste perfect course guidelines]
#end perfect course guidelines#

Provide me with a course structure in tabular format containing:

Section, Lesson title, Brief description, Lesson learning outcome, length of lesson in minutes, total cumulative course length

Plug in your Title, Topic, Total Length and the guidelines created in Part 1 about creating a perfect course.

Prompt Output

ChatGPT will create a table of your course's structure. This will be very long - so here's just a sample of the top of my table:

Section	Lesson Title	Brief Description	Lesson Learning Outcome	Length of Lesson (Min)	Cumulative Course Length (Min)
1	Introduction to AI and ChatGPT	Understand the fundamentals of AI and ChatGPT	10	10	
	Understanding Generative AI	Dive into the concept of Generative AI	Grasp the concept of Generative AI	10	20
	Overview of OpenAI	Introduction to OpenAI and its mission	Understand the vision and mission of OpenAI	10	30
	Quiz 1	-	-	10	40
2	Introduction to GPT-4	Deep dive into GPT-4 and its capabilities	Understand GPT-4	10	50
	GPT-4 in Action	Showcase of GPT-4 in real world scenarios	Understand the application of GPT-4	10	60
	Comparing GPT-4 and ChatGPT	Understanding the similarities and differences between GPT-4 and ChatGPT	Identify the pros and cons of GPT-4 and ChatGPT	10	70

3. Manual edit

Remember in the last Part where I suggested choosing a topic you are familiar with and have skill in? Here's why.

Now you need to go through the structure you've been provided and give feedback to ChatGPT

For example in the image above I see a lesson called "Comparing GPT-4 and ChatGPT".

That's not a helpful lesson - GPT-4 is a version of ChatGPT which means this comparison isn't a helpful one. I'd want to drop this lesson.

Go through your course structure and note the lessons you want to delete. For these tell ChatGPT to drop or delete these lessons.

For other sections and lessons you might want to reorder the content. Again, just type this into ChatGPT ("reverse the order of lesson x and lesson y").

For some you may think ChatGPT hasn't added enough detail or has too much detail. Ask it to add or subtract extra lessons until it's a bit more balanced.

This editing process is crucial to make your course valuable and needs to be done by you, a human expert. Thankfully editing a course outline is much easier than creating it from scratch.

4. Flesh out details

Once you've got your basic structure in a place you are happy with we're going to flesh out the details of each lesson.

We don't want to do this before the editing as we'll just end up with lots more information we need to get rid of later.

Use this nice simple prompt after your existing structure:

> *For each lesson add 3 main content bullet points.*
>
> *Add these into the existing table.*

Prompt Output

Here's a snippet:

3	Basics of Prompt Engineering	What is prompt engineering?, Importance of prompt engineering, Strategies for designing prompts
	Designing Simple Prompts	Anatomy of a simple prompt, Best practices, Hands-on exercise
	Working with Complex Prompts	What makes a prompt complex?, Strategies for handling complexity, Hands-on exercise

This is a nice simple prompt that will give you more detail on each of the lessons that ChatGPT has added into the structure.

Again, go through and manually tweak, asking ChatGPT to add/delete or edit as required.

The more we do now with our structure the better our results in the next part where we start to generate content.

Pulling it together

This part has been big but hopefully the one large prompt I've provided will do a lot of the heavy lifting.

You still had to edit based on your own knowledge but doing so is easier than working from a blank page.

And rest assured that any editing work you've just done will pay back dividends in the next Part when we start to generate content. The more specific and focused your structure the more unique and engaging our final course content.

Speaking of - that's the next topic! For that, I'll see you on the next page!

Course Scripts

In this part we're going to be focusing on fleshing out our course outline and generating the scripts.

Initially I did build you a GIANT prompt that would automatically plough through your structure and pump out individual lesson script.

It was a thing of beauty. So complex. So complete. It would have made this process *real* fast and hands-off.

The problem: the scripts it made were rubbish! ChatGPT made perfectly *fine* scripts but they were not interesting or engaging enough for the limelight.

Instead I've come up with a workflow that takes a little longer (sorry!) but outputs far higher quality course scripts.

1. Rough draft

First we're going to generate a rough first pass of a script. We're going to do this one at a time because the following steps will make your final script far superior to batch production.

Here's the prompt:

> Act as an online course expert
>
> Create a video script for [lesson] title
>
> The lesson should be [x] minutes long
>
> Using the information from above
>
> Provide image/video suggestions
>
> Provide timecodes

Use this below the rest of your work from Part 2 so that ChatGPT knows the full lesson details. If you've lost those details copy paste them into a new chat then use this prompt.

I've suggest adding in the length of the video manually because ChatGPT was extremely inconsistent here. Adding it manually overrides any inconsistency.

Otherwise, simply plug in the title and ChatGPT will do the rest.

Prompt Output

Scene 1 *(00:00 - 00:10)*
[Video starts with upbeat music, a title card appears "Showcase of GPT-4 in Real World Scenarios"]
Narrator (Voice-over): "Welcome to today's lesson where we will be showcasing the power of GPT-4 in real world scenarios."

Scene 2 *(00:10 - 00:40)*
[Show visuals of AI applications in various industries]
Narrator (Voice-over): "The AI revolution is upon us. Its influence spans across industries, from healthcare to finance, and today, we will witness how GPT-4 is contributing to this revolution."

Scene 3 *(00:40 - 01:30)*
[Show visuals of content creation with AI: blogs, scripts, articles]
Narrator (Voice-over): "First up, let's talk about content creation. GPT-4 can generate human-like text, making it a powerful tool for creating blogs, scripts, and even books. Let's look at some examples."

2. Manual edits

ChatGPT will give us a basic draft of a script, hitting the learning outcomes and main points that we set up in the structure in Part 2.

If you just used this script the end result of the course would be...underwhelming.

It would feel like a course written by ChatGPT. And we don't want that!

Instead we'll use the first draft that has been generated and tell ChatGPT to make adjustments. Use your knowledge of the subject here.

For instance I got a lesson that including topics that I think are too detailed:

> **Scene 3** (00:40 - 01:20)
> [Show screen recording of OpenAI API documentation]
>
> **Narrator (Voice-over):** "Before we start, make sure you have access to OpenAI's API. If you haven't, follow the instructions on their documentation page to get started."
>
> **Scene 4** (01:20 - 02:30)
> [Show code editor with Python script]
>
> **Narrator (Voice-over):** "Let's start with writing a Python script. First, import the necessary libraries. We'll be using OpenAI's Python library for this project."
>
> [Narrator explains the code]

API and Python would be too complex for the course I am designing. Therefore I'd simply tell ChatGPT this.

In this case I'd add a new prompt saying "API and Python are too complex for this course. Rewrite this lesson without reference to these topics".

ChatGPT would then rewrite, hitting the same learning objectives and main points but without mentions of APIs and coding languages like Python.

This is just an example - you'll need to read through and make similar suggestions directly to ChatGPT based on your knowledge of the subject matter.

Do this as your first pass of the script before moving onto the next steps where we refine the lessons.

3. Metaphors

The first refinement we want to add is the use of metaphors.

When you have the basic content of the script in place via manual editing - and not before! - we want to ask ChatGPT to come up with a nice metaphor to encapsulate the meaning of the lesson.

This is a teaching technique that will make the content easier to consume. You don't need to use this on all lessons but definitely try it on the more complex or abstract lessons you create.

Use this prompt:

> *Encapsulate the main point of this lesson in a metaphor that will aid the learner's comprehension and retention*
>
> *add this metaphor into the script and give me an updated version of the script.*

In the following output this was the initial version:

Scene 1 *(00:00 - 00:10)*
[Video starts with upbeat music, a title card appears "Showcase of GPT-4 in Real World Scenarios"]
Narrator (Voice-over): "Welcome to today's lesson where we will be showcasing the power of GPT-4 in real world scenarios."

Scene 2 *(00:10 - 00:40)*
[Show visuals of AI applications in various industries]
Narrator (Voice-over): "The AI revolution is upon us. Its influence spans across industries, from healthcare to finance, and today, we will witness how GPT-4 is contributing to this revolution."

Prompt Output

Which leads to this version with metaphor added:

Scene 1 *(00:00 - 00:20)*
[Video starts with upbeat music, a title card appears "Showcase of GPT-4 in Real World Scenarios"]
Narrator (Voice-over): "Welcome to today's lesson. Let's imagine GPT-4 as a master key. Just as a master key unlocks numerous doors, GPT-4 opens a myriad of possibilities in different scenarios."

Scene 2 *(00:20 - 00:50)*
[Show visuals of AI applications in various industries]
Narrator (Voice-over): "The AI revolution is upon us. And today, using our master key - GPT-4, we will unlock the doors to various real-world applications."

Don't like the metaphor ChatGPT uses? Ask for another.

Or, ask for a specific type of metaphor.

You can have some fun with this - here for instance is a nautical metaphor:

> **Scene 1** *(00:00 - 00:20)*
> [Video starts with upbeat music, a title card appears "Showcase of GPT-4 in Real World Scenarios"]
> **Narrator (Voice-over)**: "Welcome aboard our voyage of discovery! Today, we're sailing the expansive ocean of AI with our ship, GPT-4, set to explore various islands of opportunity."
>
> **Scene 2** *(00:20 - 00:50)*
> [Show visuals of AI applications in various industries]
> **Narrator (Voice-over)**: "In the vast sea of the AI revolution, our ship, GPT-4, enables us to navigate through a myriad of real-world applications."
>
> **Scene 3** *(00:50 - 01:40)*
> [Show visuals of content creation with AI: blogs, scripts, articles]
> **Narrator (Voice-over)**: "Our first island is the Land of Content Creation. Here, GPT-4 proves to be a capable wordsmith, crafting human-like text for blogs, scripts, and even books."

4. Frameworks/Acronyms

Another way we can increase engagement and retention of our material is by putting information into frameworks with easy to remember acronyms.

What do I mean by this?

One of the most famous example is SMART goals. This is a framework for goal setting where goals are:

- **S**pecific.
- **M**easurable.
- **A**chievable.
- **R**elevant.
- **T**ime-bound

ChatGPT is really good at coming up with frameworks once it has your information.

I've got one for ChatGPT prompt engineering that I use in my material: RISEN.

- **Role:** The role or entity you want the AI to simulate.
- **Instruction:** Commands or instructions given to the AI.
- **Steps:** Sequence the AI should follow if applicable.
- **End goal:** The desired result from the AI's response.
- **Narrowing:** Constraints such as length, tone, etc. within which the AI should operate.

Whilst I had the basics of this framework in my head it was ChatGPT that helped me come up with the acronym that makes it much easier for students to learn.

> *Act as an education specialist*
>
> *Analyse the lesson in the script and construct a framework into which to put the information*
>
> *Apply single letters to each piece of the framework so that an acronym is formed. The acronym must be a word.*

I'm going to apply this to a lesson on Pro Tips for Using ChatGPT.

Prompt Output

 The framework that can be created to encapsulate the information in the lesson is as follows:

1. **U**nderstanding: The basic knowledge of what prompt engineering is and how it is used in AI.
2. **S**trategy: The strategies and techniques employed in prompt engineering, such as the RISEN framework and being specific with prompts.
3. **E**xamples: Illustrative examples of how these strategies can be effectively employed.
4. **R**eiteration: The practice of trial and error to improve results.

These key aspects of the lesson can be remembered using the acronym **USER**, where U stands for Understanding, S for Strategy, E for Examples, and R for Reiteration. This acronym represents the learner as the 'user' of AI, fitting for the context of the lesson.

This is nice little acronym as it's also about users, who are the people "using" ChatGPT! That works nicely.

Even more powerfully you can ask ChatGPT to come up with more variations. One such variation would be **FACE**, where F stands for Fundamentals, A for Approach, C for Cases, and E for Experimentation.

Alternatively if you like most of the acronym but one letter doesn't work for you just ask for an alternative for that letter. The rest will be kept the same.

Including these sort of frameworks (and acronyms) is most powerful in lessons where there is a sequence of instructions you want the learner to be able to remember.

These sort of frameworks are also great because they'll be your intellectual property (IP) - they are unique ways of presenting information that you can use in your courses, eBooks, blog, newsletter and social media. They are extremely powerful IP assets.

5. Compiling your scripts

Once you are happy with the script for your first lesson we need to copy/paste it somewhere safe.

I personally use Notion. It's free and an excellent place to organise information for projects like this.

Here for example is my Notion for a (work-in-progress!) course on using ChatGPT:

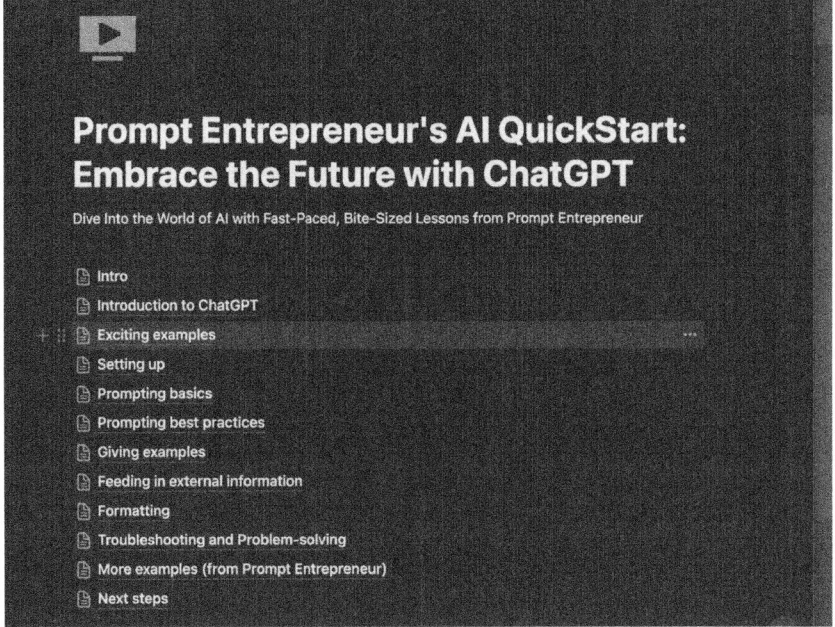

Each of those entries like Intro, Setting Up etc. are sections of my course

Each section has separate lesson documents inside it:

Prompting best practices

- P - Precise: Make your instructions clear and precise. Vague questions or prompts ma...
- R - Relevant: Keep your prompts relevant to the topic at hand. The model doesn't rem...
- I - Iterative: If you're not getting the response you desire, refine and iterate your prom...
- M - Moderate: Moderation is key. Extremely lengthy or complex prompts may confuse...
- E - Explicit: Ensure that the expected format of the response is explicitly indicated in t...

You can also just use Notes or a Google Doc but Notion allows you to have a hierarchy of Course > Sections > Individual Lessons.

Once you've decided where to keep your scripts simply copy/paste them out of ChatGPT, saving them into your note taking system of choice.

We'll need to come back to them in the next step when we create our videos and having them all organised neatly now will save huge amounts of time. You don't want to be searching for each lesson's script in ChatGPT!

Pulling it together

In this part we've looked at how we flesh out a script and get it to a place where we are happy with its quality. I've also added in tips on adding metaphor or building a learning framework into the lesson to really up its value.

Your job now is to run this process with each of the lessons in your course.

This may take a little time - depending on the length of your course.

Remember though the alternatives. Either:

- Writing everything from scratch. Very time consuming.
- Auto generating everything from ChatGPT. Poor quality.

Instead we are leveraging ChatGPT and our knowledge to find a happy medium of speed and quality.

Next up we're pushing on to the actual creation where we turn these scripts into videos.

Course recording and editing

In this part we're going to finally start to put together our videos for our online course.

We've done a lot of prep to get to this point to make sure that our content is actually good quality.

There's no point spending time producing videos of crappy content. Therefore we focused on nailing the *script first*.

I used to produce TV/Film and you definitely want to work out the kinks when it's pen and paper and not video files! Scripts are a lot easier to work with than video footage believe me!

Let's get started.

1. Choice of production tools

Video production is a HUGE topic.

So I've been struggling to break this down into my usual "here's exactly what to do" approach.

This is make even more true by the fact that I want to balance your time and money input. For some people using paid for tools to produce video will be an efficient use of money. Whereas for others using free tools and putting in more personal work will be the answer.

I've debated this! I really have.

Here's the deal. I'm going to run through the options now and give you one that I'm choosing to detail.

I'll give you reasons and also more resources to use other tools if you aren't happy. It's hard to please everyone here so I'm aiming for the majority!

Options

a) The first method is to record and edit manual.

I've done this before, notably on my https://learnchinesecharacters.academy/ videos as well as my early Udemy courses.

The basic steps are:

- make a slide deck from your script in Powerpoint or Keynote
- screen record yourself going through the slides on a webcam using a tool like Loom
- edit using a free editor like iMovie, adding in stock videos and imagery from free sources like Pexels (https://www.pexels.com/) and stocksnap.io.

This is entirely doable and uses free or low price tools.

The main cost is instead your time.

I've done this process a few times and creating a video course takes months.

b) Descript

Descript (https://www.descript.com/) is an amazing tool for recording and editing. It's a complete suite of tools that can replace all the free versions I mentioned above.

Basically, creating a course in Descript would be the more premium version of the manual approach above. It costs about $12 or $24 dollars a month for the version of Descript you would need.

It still requires lots of work but the tool itself makes each sub-process smoother. You can expect to turn out a course in a couple of weeks.

c) Pictory

Pictory (<https://pictory.ai/>) is a new kid on the block and uses AI to produce videos much faster than if you were manually putting them together.

You upload your script and it automatically picks out suitable videos and images, adds written subtitles and generates AI voice over.

It has a free trial to play with and costs $19-39/month for a premium account, depending on how much you need to export.

d) Synthesia

Synthesia (<https://www.synthesia.io/>) is the "big boy" in AI video generation. It produces high quality corporate style videos, including custom AI avatars who can present your course like a real human being.

The quality of Synthesia is extremely high. As is the price. There's no free trial and the paid account is ~$30/month for 10 credits. Each credit gets you 1 minute of video! So we're talking $3/minute.

Wowzers.

Which to use?

These are a few of the big options you have.

If you have zero cash to invest into this then the choice is easy - you'll need to go with the manual free route.

However, we're Prompt Entrepreneurs. We want to use the best AI tools available to us to get the work done efficiently.

As such this Part of the guide will be focusing on using Pictory.

This will allow you to create your whole course in a matter of days for ~$40, a sum of money that will be quickly recouped once you launch your course.

2. Video first draft

First up head over to *Pictory* to sign up.

It has a free trial. Yay!

It also doesn't need a credit card. Double yay!

You can sign up at *https://pictory.ai/*

Once in you'll see this:

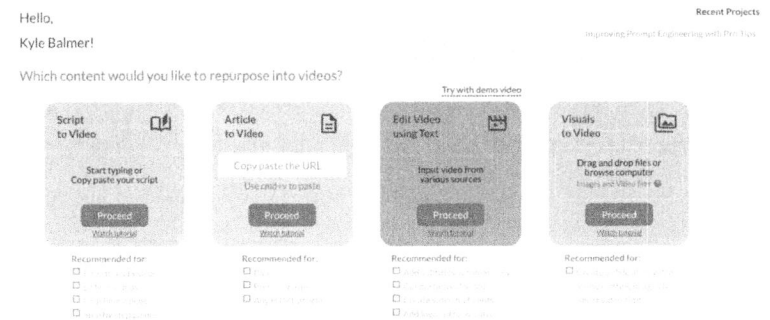

We want to go for **Script to Video**. Go ahead and click Proceed and you'll get the script editor.

Here it is with a script that I've copy pasted in.

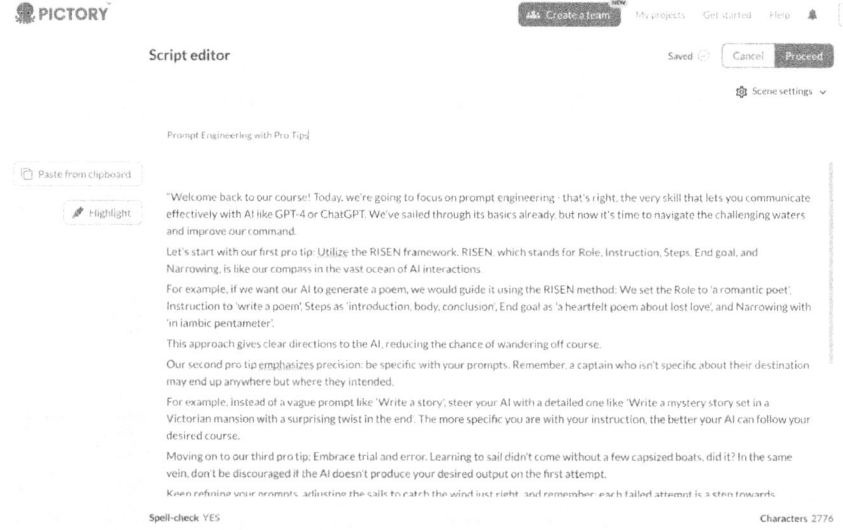

Notice that I've stripped the timecodes and description out of the script.

The scripts we have prepared, complete with image suggestions and time codes, are fleshed out enough to be used in any format. The extra detail will be invaluable in manual editing in particular. When using AI tools like Pictory though we'll just strip that info out quickly.

Go ahead and drop your script into ChatGPT and use the prompt:

> *Give me this script but remove timecodes and images suggestions*
>
> *Provide spoken script only*

Copy this stripped down version of the script into Pictory and hit Proceed.

Next, Pictory will give you a selection of templates. Don't sweat this too much as we can change it in the editor later. It's not final so just choose one you like the look of for now.

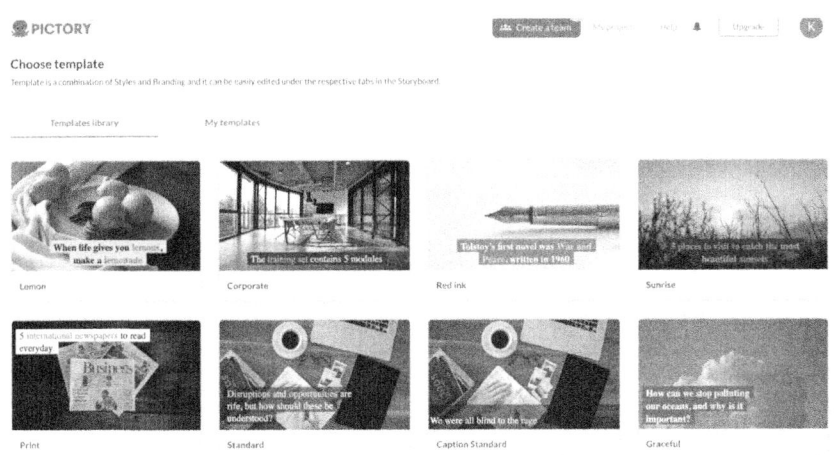

Pictory will now process the video. It doesn't take long - less than a minute. Once done it will spit out a first draft:

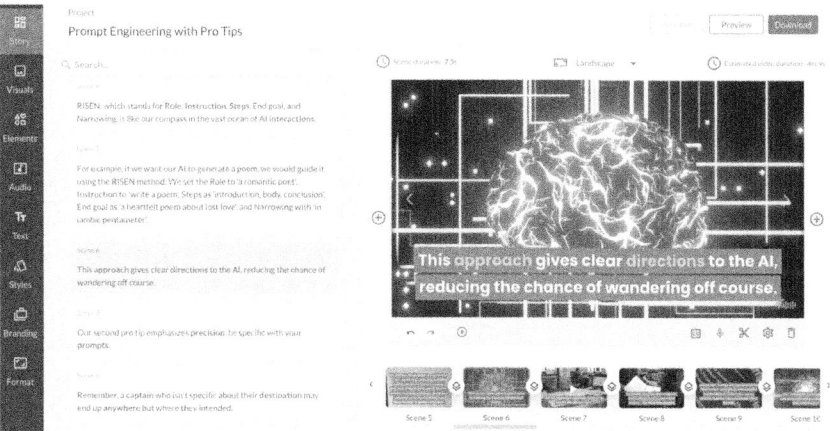

If you've ever manually prepared video content then chances are right now that your mind is blown.

Compared to manually preparing a similar video the speed Pictory works at is phenomenal.

Remember though: this is a first draft.

Like with all AI tools we're working with the tool. We aren't totally replacing ourselves.

3. Refining the video

The left sidebar in Pictory gives us access to the tools to refine our video. Take some time to explore the interface.

First we'll start by switching out images that don't make sense. Pictory will make a best guess about what videos and images to place in the video but sometimes it gets it wrong or the images are uninteresting.

Here's an example:

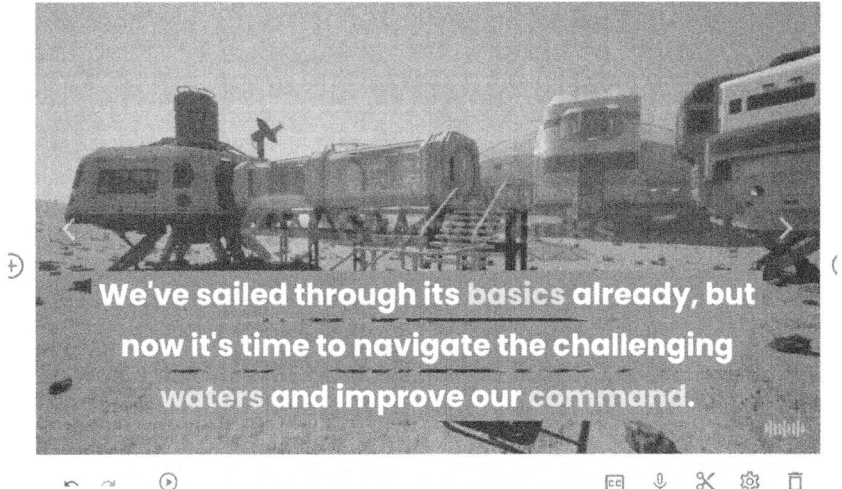

This part of the video is about moving from easy topics to more challenging topics. For some reason Pictory has chosen a video of a Martian space base. Let's switch that out.

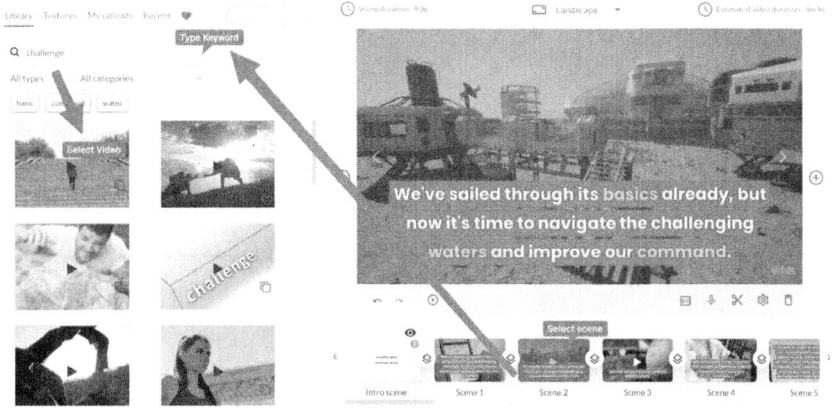

To switch this:

- Select the Scene at the bottom
- Type a keyword in the top left search bar within Library
- Select the video you want to use

This automatically switches the video and cuts the new video to length so it fits in the same Scene.

Do this for each of the Scenes until you are happy with the overall results.

Next up, we want to add a voice over.

It's decision time now. You can either use one of Pictory's built in AI voices or record your own narration.

If you have a decent audio setup (a microphone or at least high quality headphones like Airpods) and you are comfortable recording you should.

AI voice-overs save a lot of time but aren't particularly engaging. They sound like AIs! The technology is improving all the time though.

Test out Pictory's built in AIs and see what you think. Also record some of your own narration so you can do a comparison.

Here's how to record narration:

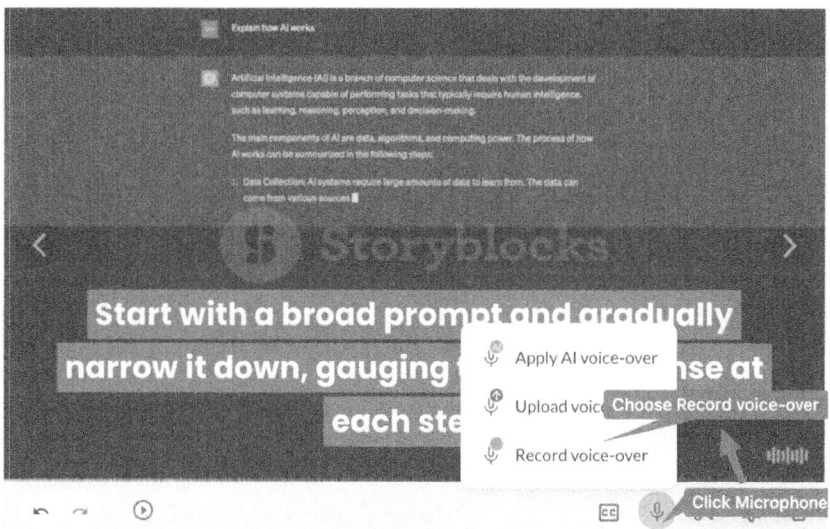

First click the microphone icon at the bottom of a selected Scene. Then choose Record Voice-over.
This will pop up a recording interface where you can record.

Importantly Pictory will match this up with the scene, saving you time trying to synch audio and video. Another massive time saver.

Speaking of sound, you probably have noticed that Pictory has chosen some **background music.**

If you don't want any music go to the Audio tab in the left sidebar then Background music. You'll see one music track has the word "Applied" next to it. To clear that music click the cross (x) to delete.

Alternatively you can replace the music with something more fitting. There are drop downs for selecting mood, purpose, genre and length. You can use these to filter the large music library and find something appropriate.

Generally it helps to have some music in the background and it fills empty space between narration. Just make sure that the volume isn't overpowering compared to the narration. Pictory does a good job of balancing thankfully.

Finally, some of you might be wanting to add your beautiful faces into the video. There's a nice simple way to do this. Just record the scene you want to replace using your camera, speaking the part of of the script in that scene. Then replace the visuals in that scene with the video and turn off any AI narration.

Once you've got the video customised hit the Preview button. That will show you the results of your work with all the changes applied.

Don't export just yet though!

4. Branding and export

Before you export your videos it's helpful to set up branding for your course. This branding will be applied across all your videos so it's helpful to set this up before you start exporting any videos.

Branding is set up in the left hand sidebar tab

Branding. Good name eh?

We specifically want an Intro and Outro.

Keep them extremely short, maybe 1 or 2 seconds tops. These should simply state the title of the lesson and have a quick animation.

For the Intro follow these steps:

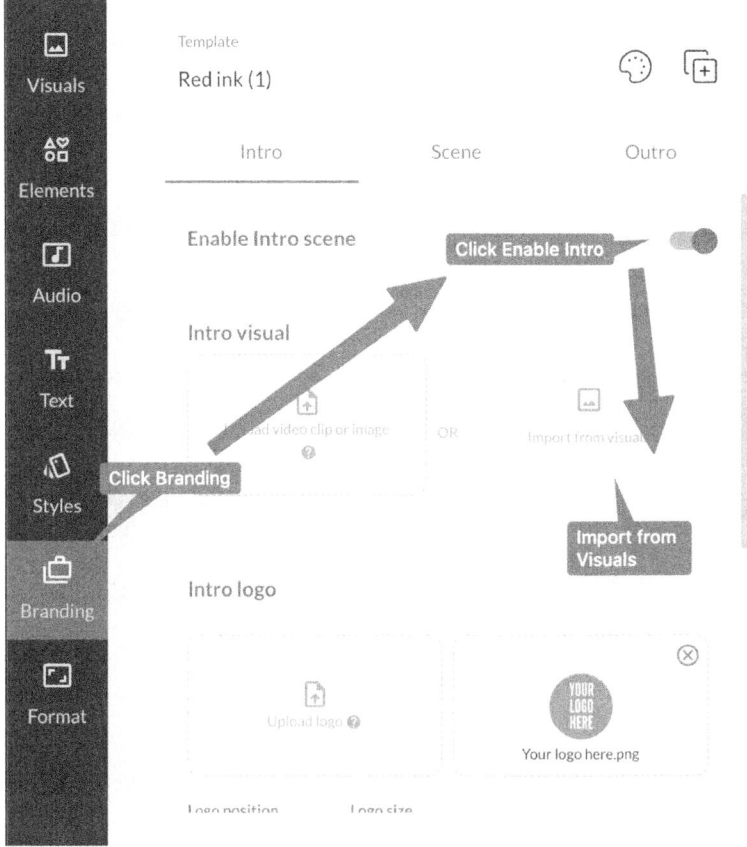

First go to Branding in the left sidebar.

Then Enable Intro toggle on.

There may already be an intro template in place. Delete the default and choose Import from Visuals.

This will take you to the video search we used before to find visuals for our Scene.

Here's a clever tip: now just search "intro" and you'll get lots of nice background animations.

Once you've found one you like make sure to edit the Title (text is at the bottom) and upload your logo.

Do the same with the Outro but searching "outro" in the search. Or alternatively use the same animation as the intro.

Alternatively you can get intro and outro videos professionally made on *Fiverr.com* for a reasonable cost. This would be a good investment to increase the quality of your production very cost effectively.

Now go back to the Preview and check the results. Happy? Go ahead and export.

The free version will allow you to export a limited number of projects and they will all have water marks - so you will need a paid version eventually.

Just rest assured that you have saved thousands of dollars in hours by using an efficient tool like this.

Also, if you get all your videos processed in 30 days you only need to pay for one month. Not bad!

Pulling it together

Seems like a lot in this part.

But considering we covered a topic as complex as video creation this is pretty tight! This topic could have taken up the whole week if we were doing it the old way.

I for one am glad to not have to be making Powerpoint slide decks and screen recording everything in real time. Tools like Pictory make the process much faster - especially if it's your first time producing a course.

Instead of being a course creator and video producer you can focus on the course itself and let the technical parts be handled by tech.

Production will still take time, especially if you follow the Refinement steps outlined above. But course creation is now in hand and can begin.

We're moving into the back end of the process now. Next we look at packaging everything up, getting it published on Udemy and marketing.

Course Marketing

In the final Part of this guide we're going to finalise our course and set it up for success on Udemy.

Most of the marketing will be done by Udemy themselves once we have published the course.

However it's useful to get some early good reviews on your course to help it become more visible on Udemy. For this we'll do a little external marketing in addition to relying on Udemy.

1. Course Setup and Curriculum

We're going to let Udemy do the majority of the marketing for us.

Remember that this is why we chose to use Udemy rather than building a course on YouTube or a self hosted website.

This is because Udemy has a built in audience and will push your course for you.

But to make sure Udemy shows your course to its audience we need to ensure we've filled in as many details as possible about our course and optimised our course description.

First let's get our course online.

Log into the Udemy Instructor's interface. We created an Instructor's account back in Part 1 so refer to that if you don't yet have an account.

The majority of the set up process is simple: Udemy has a great course creation tool that walks you through everything you need to do.

First up hit New Course and start to fill in the basic details. You created a course title previously - go ahead and use that. For category just choose the one closest to your topic.

The main course creation interface looks like this :

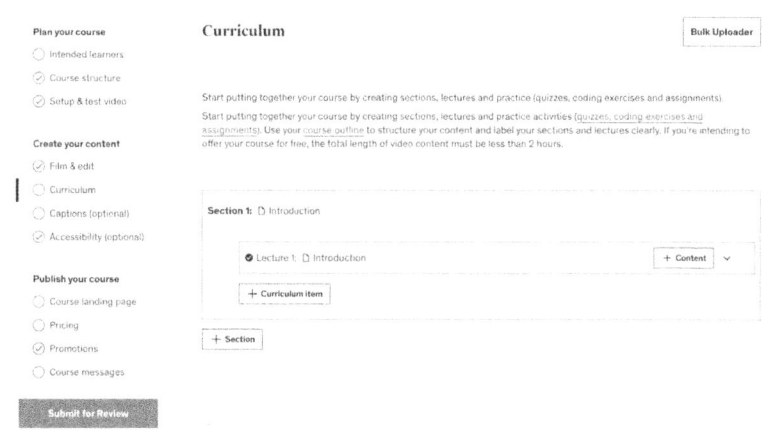

On the left you'll see the steps required.

You've already Planned your course and filmed everything so the first entry you'll be interested in will be **Curriculum** (shown in image).

In this interface you can import all of your content.

For simplicity I recommend

- Creating and naming all your sections as per your course structure
- Creating and naming all your lessons
- Bulk uploading all your videos using the bulk upload tool
- Assigning videos to each lesson
- Add descriptions for each lesson from the course structure

Refer back to the course structure we created in ChatGPT for all the text details you need. This includes the lesson description - just copy paste in the descriptions from the ChatGPT course structure table.

This process still takes some time but thankfully you have everything ready in a nicely formatted table.

Additionally if you titled your videos in Pictory your video file names will have the same lesson title. This makes assigning videos to lessons much faster.

2. Create Quizzes

This step is optional but adds a lot of value.

In Udemy you can add quizzes to reinforce student learning. This isn't required but it adds a lot of value to your course and increases engagement.

Crucially we also have a tool to help us make quizzes!

Udemy accepts multiple-choice quizzes. You can either make quizzes for every lesson or just one for each section - it's up to you.

To make a lesson quiz use this prompt

> *Act as a teacher.*
>
> *Analyse this lesson and give me 3 multiple choice questions that would reinforce student learning.*
>
> *Provide the question and 3 potential answers per question, 1 right, 2 wrong.*
>
> *Write a description of the quiz*
>
> *#copy/paste lesson script#*

Prompt Output

Quiz Description:

This short quiz aims to reinforce your understanding of the concepts we discussed in the lesson 'Improving Prompt Engineering with Pro Tips'. The questions below will challenge your knowledge about the RISEN framework, the importance of precision in prompts, the trial and error approach, and the limitations of AI. Good luck!

Question 1: What does the acronym RISEN stand for in the context of prompt engineering?

A. Response, Instruction, Sequence, Example, Narrowing
B. Role, Instruction, Steps, End goal, Narrowing
C. Result, Input, Steps, Example, Numbers

Question 2: What was one of the key takeaways regarding the use of prompts in AI interactions?

A. Being vague and general in prompts often yields the best results.
B. It's best to avoid trial and error and get the perfect prompt at the first attempt.
C. Being specific and detailed in prompts improves the output.

Question 3: Which of the following statements is a limitation of GPT-4 or similar AI models?

A. AI models like GPT-4 can access real-time data and provide current, up-to-date information.
B. AI models like GPT-4 cannot produce human-like text.
C. AI models like GPT-4 cannot access real-time data or provide current, up-to-date information.

Correct Answers:
Question 1 - B,
Question 2 - C,
Question 3 - C.

Then simply copy paste these quiz outputs into the Udemy interface.

If you want to do one quiz per Section (instead of per lesson) then adapt the prompt so suggest one question per lesson and provide all the scripts below the prompt.

3. Landing Page

Next up is the landing page. This is the most impactful part of our Udemy marketing.

Our landing page text is where we performs SEO (search engine optimisation) to ensure we show up in Udemy.

We're going to pull in information from multiple places to write this text.

Here's the prompt:

> Act as a SEO copywriter
>
> Write a course description that will be on a landing page for my course on Udemy.
>
> The goals are SEO visibility and an accurate description for potential customers.
>
> Focus on these keywords : [udemy keywords]
>
> Build upon this course basic description [description]
>
> Include this course structure [course structure]
>
> Include learning outcomes.
>
> Use formatting including bold, italics, numbered lists and bullet points

Generate at least 2000 words of description.

It's a big prompt pulling from multiple sources. This ensures the output will be unique and tailored to your course.

Plug in details from previous parts. As much as possible.

You may find that ChatGPT can't handle all the information in one go - this will depend on how long your course and all its structure is.

If this is the case copy paste the prompt in and immediately hit enter. Don't fill in any missing details. ChatGPT will then ask you for the missing details.

This allows you to add details piece by piece so you won't hit limitations.

Prompt Output

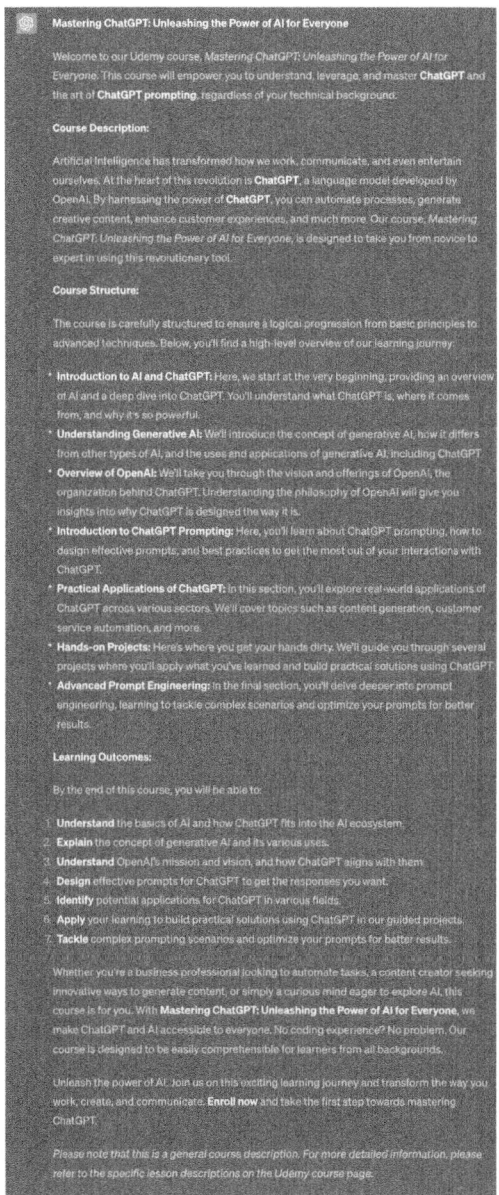

As always read the output and ask for changes as required.

This is the main element of your landing page covered - it's the course description that most determines search-ability.

For your course image I recommend Canva - just make sure to match Udemy's required image size.

Alternatively you can easily hire someone on Fiverr to do a course image for low cost.

4. Instructor Bio

Next is your instructor bio.

Writing about yourself can be hard so I've written up a script that will coach you through the process and generate a bio.

> You are a brand manager who works with educators. You will help me write a bio about myself by guiding me through a set of questions.
>
> Ask these questions sequentially, not at the same time. Once you have collected an answer from me continue to the next question. Continue until all questions have been answered and then prepare the bio.
>
> The questions are:
>
> -name and main occupation ?
> -professional experience in the field you are teaching ?
> -personal hobbies and interests related to field you are teaching
> -what brought you to udemy to teach?
> -how will you best help your students?
>
> Once the questions have been answered you will prepare a professional yet approachable bio, written in the first person, intended to make people trust me and want to buy my courses.

> *End with a gentle call to action to enrol in one of my courses*

Once initiated ChatGPT will ask questions - just work through the questions and give as much information as possible.

At the end ChatGPT will generate a bio containing all the information.

Prompt Output

 Thank you for sharing, Kyle.

Now, let's create your bio.

Hello, I'm Kyle, a digital marketer with two decades of experience in the field. Along with holding an MBA, I have spent a significant portion of my career building online businesses, giving me a unique perspective on the challenges and opportunities you might face. My interests also extend into the realm of artificial intelligence (AI), and I'm passionate about exploring how these advanced technologies can transform the digital marketing landscape.

While I've run numerous in-person workshops and authored several books, I realized that I wanted to reach an even wider audience. That's why I've chosen Udemy as my platform to teach digital marketing. It gives me the opportunity to connect with learners from around the world, just like you.

My main aim as an educator is to ensure that all my students, regardless of their level of experience, feel confident and well-equipped in the field of digital marketing. This includes providing easy-to-understand AI lessons that you can practically apply in starting your own business.

If you're ready to start your journey in the world of digital marketing, or even if you're looking to expand your existing knowledge, you're in the right place. Join one of my courses today and let's explore the fascinating, ever-evolving world of digital marketing together.

Looking forward to seeing you in class!

5. Pricing

Choosing a price on Udemy can be tricky.

Here's the key though:

90%+ or Udemy sales are at a discount from the price you put - nearly nobody buys a course at full price. Instead Udemy constantly discounts courses.

This may seem annoying but it's the key to selling at volume!

It also means we set a high price, knowing it will be discounted.

For your price I recommend you first check competitors and their pricing bracket. Find courses that are a similar length to yours.

Now, take your price down 1-2 brackets from their price.

Why? Because you have zero reviews! They can sell for more because they have lots of happy customers and social proof - you don't yet.

So for now use their pricing as a guide and knock down 1-2 price brackets. Once you have a good amount of reviews you can increase the price.

6. Getting the word out

We chose Udemy specifically because they take care of most of the marketing.

However, it's useful to "prime the pump" and get some early positive reviews.

If you already have social media, blog, newsletter, podcast or other audiences great! You just need to make sure they know about your new course. I'm not going to worry about you guys too much as you already have a following!

If you don't have a following yet here are a couple of options.

First up, tell *me* about your course on Twitter. If you prepared it using this guide I want to help you out. I've got an audience and will use your course as a case study - that helps get the word out.

Second, tell family and friends. You can get your first handful of sales here easily. For launch set your price as low as possible (free if the course is under 2 hours) and give your friends and family members the cash to buy your course. They purchase, you reimburse. They leave a verified review. This is a nice simple way to get your first 10 or so 5 star reviews!

Third, do a community blitz. In preparation for your course launch (weeks before) find and start to participate in a community who will be interested in the course.

Where this community lives will depend entirely on your topic. Generally though there will be a community on Reddit, Twitter or LinkedIn Groups.

Begin participating, commenting, being helpful. Don't shill your course. Just become known and liked.

As you approach course launch mention that you have a course and want some feedback. Again, don't sell - genuinely seek feedback from the community.

As you approach launch maybe start to mention it's coming and offer some discount codes (Udemy allows you to do this).

Because you've only just joined this community you need to play this very cool - don't sell hard, don't spam. For the next launch make sure you have strong links or your own community!

Using one or a handful of these methods ought to get you the first handful of reviews which will help kickstart real sales.

Pulling it together

Well done for making it this far.

Recap

Boom 💥!

We've covered a lot. This is a complex topic.

Creating a course is definitely a time investment but once it's up and running it's a great passive income earner.

From here you can also branch your course out onto Skillshare, Coursera and other platforms.

And importantly you are now building an audience of students. Do what you can (within platform rules) to move your students onto your social media accounts and your newsletter if you have one.

Doing this allows you to start multiplying your business in unexpected ways. You'll find you can sell your course students your ebooks, newsletter, coaching etc. once they are in your ecosystem.

And vice versa you can sell ebook readers, newsletter subscribers and coaching clients your courses!

Whilst building each pillar of your business takes time once a handful are operational you will begin to see exponential results.

And we can use ChatGPT and other AI tools like Pictory to radically accelerate our progress!
That's all for now Prompt Entrepreneurs.

Well Done

Most don't make it this far. Remember...

AI is moving fast. Extremely fast.

So I want you to do two things:

(1) **Follow me** on Twitter: *@iamkylebalmer*

(2) **Subscribe** to my free email newsletter: Prompt Entrepreneur

Both options will keep you up-to-date and ahead of the game when it comes to AI.

I'll see you there.

PS - Amazon will ask you to review this book. It takes a serious amount of time to produce these Playbooks. My only ask is you take a couple of minutes to leave a review.

Useful Links

In this playbook I've shared various links. I've also in places used 'short links' to make it easier for you to type that URL. But sometimes these links 'break'.

Here's the full links for your reference:

My Twitter: https://twitter.com/iamkylebalmer

My Free Email Newsletter: https://promptentrepreneur.beehiiv.com/ (or https://tinyurl.com/3sp8unc4)

This book in a digital format: https://www.notion.so/Course-Creation-using-AI-76fa4f8e49144902b9d02a5fec167f73?pvs=4 (or https://tinyurl.com/4ec7c5cm)

AI Chat - ChatGPT: https://openai.com/chatgpt

AI Image creation - MidJourney: https://www.midjourney.com/home/

Email Software - Beehiiv: https://www.beehiiv.com/?via=kyle-balmer (or https://tinyurl.com/53sszm6d)

About the Author

Kyle Balmer is an established entrepreneur and renowned expert in leveraging AI for business growth. With decades of experience in launching and managing online businesses, Kyle has amassed a wealth of practical insights which he passionately shares with his audience.

He has successfully mentored over 26,000 students on Udemy, sharing his knowledge about entrepreneurship and the innovative use of AI in business. His approach to teaching focuses on the practical, guiding his students on their journey to starting and growing their own businesses.

As the author of the daily newsletter, "Prompt Entrepreneurs," Kyle provides his readers with in-depth insights into AI business models and actionable guides to generate new income streams, even for those with minimal technical skills. This daily roadmap to AI entrepreneurship has become a trusted source for many aspiring and seasoned entrepreneurs alike.

Stay connected with Kyle on Twitter (@iamkylebalmer) for real-time updates on AI developments in business and actionable tips on monetizing AI. Kyle Balmer is not just an author but a guide, helping you navigate the challenging yet exciting world of AI entrepreneurship.

Kyle studied History at Oxford University before setting off to Vietnam to set up the co-found the country's first private television station. After getting his MBA at NYU Stern in New York, Kyle moved to China to learn the "world's most difficult" language. Kyle now runs several online businesses, including those in the digital marketing, Chinese language, blockchain and AI spaces.

Other books in the series

For all upcoming AI and online business book releases be sure to subscribe to the Prompt Entrepreneur email :

"Uncover the secrets of talking to AI for online business success".

Subscriber free: https://promptentrepreneur.beehiiv.com/subscribe

Printed in Great Britain
by Amazon